# REVIVAL

A LENTEN DEVOTIONAL FOR
EUCHARISTIC RENEWAL

Copyright © 2025 National Eucharistic Congress, Inc.

All rights reserved. No part of this book may be reproduced, stored in a retrieval system, or transmitted in any form or by any means—electronic, mechanical, photocopying, recording, or otherwise—without the prior written permission of the publisher, except for brief quotations in critical reviews or articles.

Published by National Eucharistic Congress, Inc.

1717 N Street NW Ste 1
Washington, D.C. 20036
eucharisticcongress.org

ISBN: 979-8-9925498-0-5

Editor: Joel Stepanek, Zachary Keith, Ph.D.

Authors: Jane Gunther, Tanner Kalina, Zachary Keith, Ph.D., Fr. Joe Laramie, S.J., Senite Sahlezghi, Joel Stepanek, Sr. Alicia Torres

Cover Design: Casey Olson

Interior Design: Casey Olson

Printed in the United States of America

For permissions or inquiries, visit eucharisticcongress.org.

# TABLE OF CONTENTS

| | |
|---|---|
| ASH WEDNESDAY | 3 |
| FIRST WEEK OF LENT | 13 |
| SECOND WEEK OF LENT | 29 |
| THIRD WEEK OF LENT | 45 |
| FOURTH WEEK OF LENT | 61 |
| FIFTH WEEK OF LENT | 76 |
| HOLY WEEK | 92 |
| EASTER SUNDAY | 110 |
| ABOUT | 114 |

# INTRODUCTION

Revival is an ongoing work. Over the past three years, Catholics in the United States responded to the Holy Spirit's call through our bishops for a National Eucharistic Revival. The fruits of this movement have been incredible.

The heart of this revival is grassroots; it happens inside dioceses and parishes at the local level. The most crucial place where revival happens is in each of us; without an interior conversion of heart, a revival of our love in the Eucharist, and a renewed sense of excitement for sharing Jesus with others, there can be no national effort. There is no National Eucharistic Revival without an interior Eucharistic revival.

The season of Lent allows us to reflect on our interior disposition and ask the Lord for this personal, interior revival. It is one thing to gather among tens of thousands of Catholics and worship God through the liturgy, and that is important. Still, it is another to go to our parish's quiet Eucharistic Adoration chapel and be vulnerable before the Lord. We must do both.

This devotional guides reflection, prayer, and hopefully revival in your life over Lent. It was prayerfully written by a group of individuals who have been close to the National Eucharistic Revival for the past three years and is one of the fruits of their work in this vineyard. Their names are listed at the end of this book, but you will find that the entries themselves do not have an author listed. This decision is intentional; we desire you to hear God's voice through our humble words, not our own. This work is more significant than any one person, just as the work of revival is the work of many.

We've written this book as a daily devotional and recommend spending time during your day praying through the scripture readings for the day and then reading the reflection. You can easily find the daily readings online at the United States Conference of Catholic Bishops website (USCCB.org), or you can find them in your Bible, as each day provides references to the readings. If you go to Mass, you will also hear these readings proclaimed. If possible, we recommend reading the readings and reflections before the Blessed Sacrament and taking time to pray through them with our Lord. Each day will take you no longer than 15 minutes to read between the readings and the reflection.

As you begin, we are praying for you and hope that the Lord can use this small devotional to bring an interior revival, which is at the heart of the National Eucharistic Revival, to your life. He desires to do great work in you this Lent; we only need to step out into the desert to meet Him. Revival happens here.

# ASH WEDNESDAY
## MARCH 5TH, 2025

**READINGS**
Joel 2:12-18
Psalm 51:3-4, 5-6ab, 12-13, 14, 17
2 Corinthians 5:20–6:2
Matthew 6:1-6, 16-18

**REFLECTION**
Relationships develop over time and are nourished, famished, sustained, or destroyed by experiences of encounter.

The moments we share with another person – large and small – all shape our relationship with them for better or worse. Shallow conversations, brief interactions, small talk, and low vulnerability define acquaintances and people we do not yet trust. We keep them at arms-length, even changing our behavior and personality around them to keep from getting "too close." We can quickly contrast these surface-level relationships with those that are deep and vital to us, those that we love and to which we are closest. These people don't simply know about us, but they *know* us.

We are broken people, and when we develop relationships with other broken people, there can be disorder and dysfunction. Out of a deep desire to be known, seen, and loved, we can open ourselves up too quickly with those who have not yet earned our trust, only to be hurt when that depth of relationship is not reciprocated. We can overshare with others, oftentimes via social media. We can seek support from a vast network of avatars and screen names only to find that we are shouting into a void and wondering if anyone can hear us. We can put up walls with those we *should* be the most open with, keeping them out and refusing to be vulnerable.

This creates much of the disorder that exists in our relationships, even our relationship with Jesus.

In the Gospel, Jesus speaks about this disorder.

The words of Jesus in Matthew's Gospel go far beyond how we should engage in our Lenten practices; they challenge us to recognize the disordered ways we relate to our Lord.

Jesus desires to encounter us in the quiet, interior room of our hearts. There are moments when we pray together as a community, and it is good that we do. It is vital to be strengthened by our community and to pray as a Church, but even then, the Lord speaks individually to each of us and wishes to encounter us. In these inward places, we cannot hide from the Lord; it is where we are the most raw and vulnerable. In these places, there is no duplicity, hiding, filters, or curation. This is why Jesus wishes for us to "go to [our] inner room" when we pray and do so secretly.

This is intimacy. This is an encounter.

When our faith becomes devoid of these kinds of encounters, it begins to suffer. When we begin to replace these interior moments with Jesus for large, showy, public forms of prayer, fasting, and almsgiving, our faith withers. Jesus warns against these practices because the "reward" they bring—namely, the affirmation and praise of others—eventually rots, decays, and dies. It can easily rob us of the interior moments of prayer that require vulnerability.

The pathway to revival begins with the interior life. If we wish to share the love of Christ with the world and to let the fire of Eucharistic Revival burn brightly within us, we must begin to cultivate this interior space and let go of our desire for affirmation and praise of our faith. We must learn to quiet ourselves as we receive the Lord, especially when receiving the Eucharist, where we receive the reward of an encounter with Jesus.

Relationships are nourished through encounters, but the quality of the encounter matters.

# THURSDAY AFTER ASH WEDNESDAY
## MARCH 6, 2025

**READINGS**
Deuteronomy 30:15-20
Psalm 1:1-2, 3, 4 and 6
Luke 9:22-25

**REFLECTION**
If you weren't already feeling uneasy about the Season of Lent, Jesus spells out the depths of the deal for us in today's Gospel. He is going to suffer, die, and rise. Okay, that is a little intense, but we get it–we have the perspective of living after the fact. However, the self-denial and cross-carrying that following Jesus requires are just a lot.

Frankly, good. We must leave our comfort zone to let go of our weaknesses, pettiness, and sinful patterns. No saint was ever forged in the ashes of mediocrity. But, every saint was and is forged in the fires of self-sacrificial love. We can't be drawn into those flames unless we are willing to deny our desires for complacency, selfishness, and the status quo.

It is true that Jesus never gave in to any temptations and

never lived in a lukewarm way. But He did experience the same human struggles we do, and He knows it is hard. That is why we don't deny ourselves and pick up our cross alone—we do it with Him. The place where we are forged is present at every Mass, where we re-live with Him the Paschal Mystery. We can allow Jesus to transform our hearts so that with Him, we can live Eucharistic lives patterned after His own life of self-giving love.

*What can we let go of this Lent so that our heart has more room for Jesus to enter in?*

## FRIDAY AFTER ASH WEDNESDAY
### MARCH 7, 2025

**READINGS**
Isaiah 58:1-9a
Psalm 51:3-4, 5-6ab, 18-19
Matthew 9:14-15

**REFLECTION**
When we go to a wedding, we want to look our best. We get a fresh haircut or style our hair, find a dressy pair of shoes, iron and dry clean our clothing, and may even rent a suit or buy a new dress.

In today's Gospel, Jesus invites us to a wedding. He is the groom. He marries Himself to the Church, His bride; He does this through His passion, death, and resurrection. While it may not look like any wedding we've attended, Jesus' gift of His life to us is the model of any marriage. We prepare to celebrate at His wedding banquet in the season of Lent.

How can we prepare? During Lent, we may need to tidy up our lives, clearing out some of our accumulated clutter and bad habits. Perhaps we watch too much TV, eat too much junk food, and are lazy in our prayer life. These external preparations are essential.

At Mass today, we hear Psalm 51, "A heart contrite and humbled, O God, you will not spurn." This psalm calls us to a more profound internal preparation during Lent. Is my heart ready for the wedding feast?

A "contrite heart" means that we are sorry for our sins and want to avoid committing these sins again. Our sins may be selfishness, lying, missing Mass, or sexual sins. Going to confession during Lent is a beautiful way to renew our hearts; in confession, God 'clears out the clutter' from our hearts. It's not easy to say my sins to a priest; it requires preparation and courage. Know that the priest goes to confession, too! Everyone needs God's mercy in the sacrament of reconciliation.

In Psalm 51, a "humble heart" means your heart is like the Heart of Jesus. Jesus tells us He is "meek and humble of heart" [Matt 11:29]. He knows that God is His Father and Mary is the mother that God the Father has given Him. Through Jesus, God is our Father, and Mary is the mother that Jesus gave us. Jesus knows that His true identity is not rooted in popularity and acclaim; His heart is centered on the Father's love and doing His will.

As we begin our Lenten journey, we come before the Lord with humble and contrite hearts. We behold the Sacred Heart of Jesus, burning with love for us right now. He has invited us to His great wedding feast. We prepare our hearts in joyful anticipation. At every Mass, He feeds us with His Body and Blood, Soul and Divinity, in the Eucharist, renewing us from within. At every Mass, the priest holds up the Eucharist and proclaims, "Blessed are those called to the supper of the

Lamb!" Indeed, we are blessed, for Jesus has invited us to His wedding feast. This Lent, let's prepare for the celebration!

# SATURDAY AFTER ASH WEDNESDAY
## MARCH 8, 2025

**READINGS**
Isaiah 58:9b-14
Psalm 86:1-2, 3-4, 5-6
Luke 5:27-32

**REFLECTION**
"Why do you eat and drink with tax collectors and sinners?" It seems like the religious leaders of His time just never gave Jesus a break. We know that He didn't struggle with people-pleasing, but many of us do. It can range from depressing to enraging when it is never good enough for others, no matter how hard we try. Thankfully, Jesus gives us real hope in today's Gospel passage.

Consider the context here. Jesus just called on Matthew, the tax collector whose job was abhorred by his fellow Jews. As if that wasn't irritating enough, He then went and had dinner with Matthew and all his friends, a despised bunch. While it came across as scandalous to the religious leaders of His time, for us, this was a foreshadowing of great hope.

Let's face it: we are surrounded by fellow sinners every time we go to Mass. The modifying word that changes it all, and we could even argue it originates with this story, is "beloved." We are not hopeless sinners; we are beloved sinners. Jesus longs to be with us, to work in us to set us free from sin. Reconciliation is woven into the very fabric of the Mass. From the Penitential Rite to the Lamb of God, we open ourselves up to the transformative gift of God's mercy every time we acknowledge our human frailty. And that merciful love is the game changer we've been waiting for.

# FIRST SUNDAY OF LENT
## MARCH 9, 2025

**READINGS**
Deuteronomy 26:4-10
Psalm 91:1-2, 10-11, 12-13, 14-15
Romans 10:8-13
Luke 4:1-13

**REFLECTION**
We are quick to forget.

The feelings of the present moment fade quickly, and soon, the memory fades, as well, unless we work to remember. Children repeat math formulas and practice spelling words and vocabulary over and over so that the principles and rules become second nature in calculation and writing. Similarly, when a child breaks a rule or gets in trouble, a caring adult will walk them through the situation and help them understand what happened so it isn't repeated. It isn't uncommon to hear a parent say to a child, "Be careful on the swings… remember the last time you weren't paying attention." Our memory can fail us without repetition and reminders – often at the worst moments.

Our human tendency is to focus on the immediacy of the moment in front of us, the situation we face, and the challenges it presents. We can easily get washed away with the anxiety or excitement of "right now" unless we return to our memory.

This is the gift of maturity and experience. When we are presented with an opportunity that is "too good to be true," for example, we can lean back on times we've been taken advantage of or fallen for a scam. By doing this, we step out of excitement and into our reason. When faced with a difficult circumstance, we can remember other moments when we've been challenged and find renewed energy to face the obstacle.

In today's First Reading, Moses is in the middle of a long speech to the Israelite people. It is his "final lecture" as the people prepare to cross into the Promised Land, and he implores them to remember what God has done—in this case, through a specific ritual.

The message is simple: "Remember that God freed you because you will be tempted to turn away to other gods when things are challenging."

Moses understands something about human nature and memory: We quickly forget.

Ultimately, the people will turn away from God in adversity. They will turn to other gods that were worshipped before their arrival in the Promised Land to fit in with the neighboring nations. They will turn to different countries and rulers in times of war when they feel God has abandoned them. They will even look to their own strength by amassing armies and chariots, looking more like the Godless Egypt than the God-led Israel.

We do the same thing.

We forget about God's providence and the many ways that God has shown up for us in challenging times. We lose sight of the times when we've called on God to help us discern an important life decision, and, instead, we rely solely on the advice of others and our "gut feeling."

Jesus reveals to us another way.

Today's Gospel reading is one we are familiar with: Jesus is in the desert and tempted by Satan. Do you notice the areas in which Jesus is tempted, though? They all pick at the immediacy of the moment and the desire for quick satisfaction. Jesus is hungry, so the devil tempts Him with bread. Jesus has likely been praying and contemplating His mission, so the devil tempts Him with a vision of that mission fulfilled – all of the kingdoms of the world handed over to Jesus (without the pain and suffering the Kingship of Christ will demand). And then, finally, Satan attempts to strike at the very identity of Jesus as the Beloved Son of the Father by tempting Jesus to test the Father's providence and protection right then and there.

Do these sound familiar?

There are times when our souls are crying out for love, affection, and attention or when we are feeling negative emotions – anxiety, frustration, anger, even boredom. In those places, Satan comes to tempt us with quick fixes, but those quick fixes never satisfy us and often leave us hungrier and further away from God. When confronted with the hard work of a job, marriage, parenting, caring for our parents, or even our spiritual life, the temptation is to cut corners, cheat, or find a solution that comes without suffering. When we wonder if God is listening, we are tempted to ask God for an immediate "sign" to confirm that He is real and listening to us

And in the moments where we doubt if God cares for us, we are tempted to put our trust in something else.

Jesus' response to these temptations is to remember—He recalls the words of Scripture and refutes the temptation, refusing to be mastered by the present moment but digging into the history of what God has done.

As we enter into the Lenten season, we reflect and recall the places where our memory is short and where we have forgotten. This is why Mass is so vital as a weekly encounter with Jesus Christ. We read our shared history, recalling God's actions for His people. We are mindful of what God is doing as we approach the altar, witnessing a miracle as bread and wine are substantially transformed into the Body and Blood, Soul and Divinity, of Jesus Christ. We move forward with grace to avoid the temptations of the moment because the Mass has directed our gaze beyond the feelings of "right now" and toward the promise of forever.

We are quick to forget, but God is quick to call us to remember what He has done, is doing, and will do so that we can avoid the temptation of the moment and look toward eternity.

# MONDAY OF THE FIRST WEEK OF LENT
## MARCH 10, 2025

**READINGS**
Leviticus 19:1-2, 11-18
Psalm 19:8, 9, 10, 15
Matthew 25:31-46

**REFLECTION**
Imagine this vast field full of people of all ages, ethnicities, and abilities. A man stands before them, exuding gentle strength. He begins to speak words of truth. Those who cared for the least are invited into eternal happiness; those who turned their backs have chosen eternal aloneness.

This pithy summary of Matthew 25 gets to the heart of it all: if we want to be in the Kingdom of God forever, we need to be in loving relationships with the Lord and one another. It means we are willing to feed the hungry and give drink to the thirsty, shelter the unhoused, and spend time with those who are lonely. Incidentally, these are among the corporal works of mercy. Did you ever consider, though, that every time we go to Mass, Jesus performs these works of mercy in an analogous way for us?

He draws us into communion with the Blessed Trinity and the entire Mystical Body of Christ (every follower of Jesus who ever lived and is living today). He welcomes us into the home of our Catholic Church which He entrusted with the mysteries of our faith. He nourishes us with sacred scripture, and in a most sublime way He satisfies our hunger and quenches our thirst with His own Body and Blood, Soul and Divinity.

At the Mass, Jesus gives us what He then sends us forth to give to one another until we hear those blessed words, "Come… Inherit the kingdom prepared for you from the foundation of the world."

# TUESDAY OF THE FIRST WEEK OF LENT
## MARCH 11, 2025

### READINGS
Isaiah 55:10-11
Psalm 34:4-5, 6-7, 16-17, 18-19
Matthew 6:7-15

### REFLECTION
At some point in our lives, we will ask, "How can I pray better?" Because we are made in God's image, we sense deep down inside this need to be in relationship with Him. Prayer, simply stated, is a conversation with God. Putting oneself in the presence of the Creator of the Universe can feel daunting, but Jesus quells our fears today when He invites us to call God our Father.

He doesn't tell us not to *ask* for what we need. Jesus says *don't babble*, don't go on and on and on. We need to allow time to listen. If you take a cue from human biology, you have one mouth and two ears. Maybe God is trying to say we should listen twice as much as we speak! But isn't that consoling? God wants to talk to us, to be near us, to grow in union with us.

At every Mass, we pray the words that Jesus taught us, the "perfect prayer," the Our Father. At this point in the Mass, we are about to enter the Communion Rite. If we are properly disposed, we will receive Jesus in Holy Communion in a matter of moments. We should bear that first phrase of this sacred prayer in our hearts in those moments of communion— we are entering into a deeper relationship not only with God but with every brother and sister who join us at Mass (and indeed, every member of the Mystical Body of Christ). Together, we implored with confidence, "Our Father…" and now, God unfolds a wholehearted response to each petition of that simple prayer as He offers His entire self to us in the Eucharist.

# WEDNESDAY OF THE FIRST WEEK OF LENT
## MARCH 12, 2025

**READINGS**
Jonah 3:1-10
Psalm 51:3-4, 12-13, 18-19
Luke 11:29-32

**REFLECTION**
*Sign, sign, everywhere a sign, blockin' out the scenery, breakin' my mind. Do this, don't do that. Can't you read the sign?* Whether we admit it or not, we are always looking for a sign. Les Emmerson, the lead singer for Five Men Electric Band, wrote their most popular song, "Signs," after traveling Route 66. So many signs obscured the natural beauty along the way. And he didn't like it.

In today's Gospel, Jesus challenges all of us "sign-seekers." We miss the whole point when we look for signs instead of seeing Jesus. Just like Emmerson was upset because the signs obscured the landscape, we can unwittingly choose unhelpful signs over Jesus, the greatest sign of the Father's love for us.

It takes a humble, contrite heart to see Jesus as He is.

While the signs may be flashing and revolving all around us, competing for our attention, the steadfast presence of Jesus is the only sign that will not fade away. We learn to see Jesus most clearly when we fix our eyes upon Him in the Eucharist. Next time you attend Mass, pay attention as the priest elevates the Host during the Consecration, the Great Amen, and the Lamb of God. This is Jesus, the only "sign" you'll ever need.

# THURSDAY OF THE FIRST WEEK OF LENT
## MARCH 13, 2025

**READINGS**
Esther C:12, 14-16, 23-25
Psalm 138:1-2ab, 2cde-3, 7c-8
Matthew 7:7-12

**REFLECTION**
Jesus uses very active words to welcome us more deeply into this holy season of Lent. If you ponder the text a little more closely, you could almost say Jesus is giving us some pretty clear commands connected to some incredible promises. In our commodified world, this language can be pretty helpful on the spiritual plane because it is familiar to us: If you do this, you'll experience that. If you purchase this, then you'll enjoy it.

But Jesus' promises go infinitely beyond anything the world can offer, and we don't have to give anything. He wants us to receive.

What exactly are we asking for, seeking after, and knocking upon? That is a question each of us can bring to prayer today.

For us Catholics, the greatest gift we can ask for is union with God. The most marvelous quest we can embark upon is to know Jesus, our Lord and Savior. The most sublime door we can knock upon is the door of His Heart.

The most sure source of these great gifts is the Mass. In the Sacred Mysteries we celebrate—if only our hearts are humble and contrite—the door to intimacy, knowledge, and communion is open wide for us in Word and Sacrament. All we have to do is show up at the doorstep.

# FRIDAY OF THE FIRST WEEK OF LENT
## MARCH 14, 2025

**READINGS**
Ezekiel 18:21-28
Psalm 130:1-2, 3-4, 5-7a, 7bc-8
Matthew 5:20-26

**REFLECTION**
Anger is part of life, but it's an uncomfortable experience. Our bodies and emotions react strongly as if to say, "Something is not right here." We get angry when someone cuts us off in traffic, if the waiter brings the wrong order at a restaurant, or when our favorite team loses (especially if we feel that the loss involved some injustice or cheating). These superficial flashes of anger usually fade after a few moments, and we move on.

Jesus says, "Whoever is angry with his brother will be liable to judgment." He is speaking about a deeper kind of anger. Think of your grudges and old hurts, especially when they involve people close to you— family, friends, neighbors, or bosses. This kind of anger is a judgment: you are right, and they are wrong.

But we know that this is not always accurate. Are we so sure we are fully innocent and our enemy is entirely guilty? Have we ever considered the people who are angry at us? We may be the antagonist in someone's story… and we may not even realize it. Consider that reality momentarily: Just as we hold grudges (perhaps unjustly), someone is holding a grudge against us. This resentment and anger distort our relationships.

Jesus offers us a restoration plan. In today's Gospel, He says, "Leave your gift there at the altar; go first and be reconciled with your brother." Forgiveness and reconciliation can happen in a moment, and a heartfelt conversation can bring apology and pardon. But sometimes forgiveness takes longer. Reconciliation is like healing from an injury. A broken arm, reset by a skilled doctor, will heal– but it takes time. Do we truly desire the challenging work of forgiveness, or do we prefer the "comfort" of our grudges and resentments? Are we willing to "walk the healing path" with Jesus, the Divine Physician? What if we apologize, but the person doesn't forgive us? Or, what if the person who hurt us lives far away or has died? Jesus can touch and heal our hearts, even if the person we need to reconcile with is far away or reconciliation is impossible.

As we approach the altar to receive the Eucharist, are our hearts angry and bitter? Jesus wants to bring wholeness to your heart. Will you let Him? He can calm and heal your heart through prayer and sacraments.

At Mass, the priest says, "Lift up your hearts." The people reply, "We lift them up to the Lord." This is the true gift that we bring to the altar: our hearts. We can't lift our hearts to the Lord if they are weighed down by anger and judgment. This Lent, gaze upon the Sacred Heart of Jesus, offering His mercy. Then, we can share mercy with others.

# SATURDAY OF THE FIRST WEEK OF LENT
## MARCH 15, 2025

**READINGS**
Deuteronomy 26:16-19
Psalm 119:1-2, 4-5, 7-8
Matthew 5:43-48

**REFLECTION**
When was the last time you went up to one of your enemies and gave them a big bear hug? For 99% of us, this probably hasn't been a recent life experience. Yet, Jesus speaks of loving our enemies and *commands* us to love our enemies.

Around the world, men, women, and children are suffering the effects of war. As the death count for innocent civilians rises in Ukraine, Palestine, and the Congo–to name a few areas torn by war–the concept of loving those who are behind this violence can feel very foreign.

How often have we prayed for an end to war during the Prayers of the Faithful at Mass? Most parishes include this petition on most Sundays. But how frequently do we pray for those who are responsible for warfare and the acts of violence that come from it? Perhaps this would be a good start for us today, to begin praying for those who persecute us and those to whom we are connected in the Body of Christ, the Church. Jesus tells us to pray for our enemies, and praying sincerely for them is an act of love that can soften our hearts to desire their good, to truly love them.

Next time you go to Mass, remember to pray for those who hurt you, for those responsible for violence and war. The Mass is our greatest prayer, and when we bring our petitions to the Mass, we can unite them to the sacrifice of Jesus in a most powerful way. The very same Jesus who is our Prince of Peace.

# SECOND SUNDAY OF LENT
## MARCH 16, 2025

**READINGS**
Genesis 15:5-12, 17-18
Psalm 27:1, 7-8, 8-9, 13-14
Philippians 3:17–4:1
Luke 9:28b-36

**REFLECTION**
Imagine the moment.

A small group goes with Jesus to pray on a mountain but falls asleep while praying. Upon waking, they see Jesus, but something is different. His face shines, His clothing is dazzling white, and He speaks with two individuals. They listen to the conversation and realize that these men are Moses and Elijah - the embodiment of the Law and the Prophets.

This was one of the most profound of all the moments that Peter, James, and John shared with Jesus. It was a theophany – a vision of God Himself. It makes sense that Peter would ask to make tents – dwelling places – for Jesus, Elijah, and Moses, and his desire to remain on the mountain: they're in heaven!

The glory of God settles on the mountain as a cloud, and the voice of God speaks directly to the disciples. Who would not want to remain in this glorious moment? Who would not be struck with awe, wonder, and fear of the Lord?

Yet, in a breath, the moment fades, and Jesus remains alone.

Our lives are filled with these moments – places where we wish we could remain forever.

The family vacation where everyone got along. The job where we felt at home.

The quiet moment with a loved one after they've returned from a long trip. Our wedding day and our favorite family memory. Moments where we felt God's presence moving profoundly at Mass, on retreat, or in the silence of Eucharistic Adoration.

We want to stay there forever.

These moments change us, even though they end.

When we encounter Jesus, a change takes place within us. Peter, James, and John are different when they come down the mountain. They know Jesus more intimately, and in some ways, they also know themselves more. In understanding Jesus' identity, we learn more about our true identity.

Jesus reveals us to ourselves because He knows us perfectly. He sees through our imperfections and failings and recognizes our truest identity. He calls us back to that identity, even when we forget. To gaze upon the face of Christ humbly is to discover ourselves in clarity.

Soon, the disciples will find themselves in prayer again, but not on a mountain. Instead, they will be in a garden, and again, they will fall asleep. When they awake, they will not see the face of Jesus radiant and shining but disfigured – sweating blood and in anguish. They will not see Jesus conversing with Moses and Elijah but seemingly alone.

And we need to sit in these moments, too.

The face of the suffering Christ is as important in understanding our identity as the face of the transfigured Christ. We don't like to sit in these moments, though. Unlike the moments of glory – the Transfiguration moments - we aren't trying to make tents and remain in the garden. We must, however, become comfortable in these moments of suffering if we want to know Jesus intimately and, in doing so, know who we are. The glory of life is balanced by suffering, but something lies beyond that.

Consider that the transfigured body of Christ does not bear the wounds or marks of the crucifixion, but the resurrected body of Christ does. Peter, James, and John want to stay at the mountain because they don't realize there is more to the story. They think that the moment of the transfiguration is the end – the beginning of the new kingdom. But it is only a stop, just as our glorious moments are stops that reveal our identity to us along the way. We must go down the mountain and into the garden to behold the disfigured face of Jesus, suffering alone, and find our identity there as well. And then, through that suffering and, ultimately, death, we will encounter the glorified Christ who will reveal to us the final citizenship to which we are destined, along with our true identities.

And these moments – the mountain, the garden, and the empty tomb – are bound up for us in the Eucharist. To receive the Eucharist humbly is to gaze upon Christ and, in doing so, understand who we are, our identity, our citizenship, and the hope of eternal glory.

# MONDAY OF THE SECOND WEEK OF LENT
## MARCH 17, 2025

**READINGS**
Daniel 9:4b-10
Psalm 79:8, 9, 11 and 13
Luke 6:36-38

**REFLECTION**
Have you ever made a good investment? You found just the right commodity. You took a leap of faith. Your investment made returns. You invested more, and it continued to grow.

While not all of us have had noteworthy success in stocks, bonds, and retirement accounts, today, Jesus tells us that *if we are generous, we'll receive far more than we give.* This is true in the world of forgiveness, mercy, and gifting—whether those gifts be time, talent, or treasure.

What kind of investment does Jesus ask us to make? The investment of love. When we can see others through the eyes of love, mercy, and forgiveness, it comes far more naturally, and giving gifts is a cause for joy.

God is never outdone in generosity. When we give freely, forgive freely, and love intensely, God always blesses us above and beyond our human capacity. There is no place where we can experience the lavish generosity of God like during Mass. Here, if only our hearts are humble and contrite, we receive abundant merciful love. If properly disposed, we can enter into a profound communion with Jesus when we receive Him in Holy Communion. Ultimately, Mass is the closest we can get to Heaven on earth. If you've been looking for the apex of abundance and falling short, look no further!

# TUESDAY OF THE SECOND WEEK OF LENT
## MARCH 18, 2025

**READINGS**
Isaiah 1:10, 16-20
Psalm 50:8-9, 16bc-17, 21 and 23
Matthew 23:1-12

**REFLECTION**
There are few things more dangerous to pray for than humility. Why? Because it directly opposes the great sin most of us struggle with intensely: pride.

Pride says take the first place. Humility says to take the last place.

Pride says I am right. Humility says I can learn.

Pride says to do it my way, while humility says I can defer to others.

Pride says let them figure it out. Humility says let me help.

There are many types of pride, but many people find the most challenging form to be religious pride. Jesus calls this out in today's Gospel. The religious leaders of His time talked the talk, but they didn't walk the walk. They wanted praise and adulation, but they only merited correction.

Have you ever thought, "At least I'm going to Mass," or "I fulfill my Catholic obligations," while you are looking down on those who are not measuring up somewhere in your heart? Instead of compassion and understanding, do you condemn those you perceive as far from God?

There is good news! This Gospel is for every one of us who struggles with pride. It is impossible to be humble on our own, but with God, it is possible. It can all begin by asking Jesus to help us see Him more as we gaze upon the Sacred Host. As we slowly perceive His holy face hidden under the appearance of bread, Jesus will hone our ability to see His face hidden in our brothers and sisters who are furthest from Him. Moved with compassion, we will bring them spiritually with us to Mass and be moved in charity to walk with them on a mutual journey toward God and His great gift of salvation.

# SOLEMNITY OF SAINT JOSEPH, SPOUSE OF THE BLESSED VIRGIN MARY
## MARCH 19, 2025

**READINGS**
2 Samuel 7:4-5a, 12-14a, 16
Psalm 89:2-3, 4-5, 27, 29
Romans 4:13, 16-18, 22
Matthew 1:16, 18-21, 24a

**REFLECTION**
Wouldn't it be nice if there were no twists and turns on the path to Heaven? Alas, this pilgrim journey Home is full of ups and downs, detours, and even dead ends for all of us. But, we walk by faith, one of God's greatest gifts.

With that in mind, consider St. Joseph, the man entrusted to love and serve the Virgin Mother and the Son of God. If you've ever felt like you didn't measure up to a task, imagine what Joseph experienced internally as he heard the angel assure him in a dream that God's plan was unfolding in his midst. Not only was Mary to be his wife, but through the Holy Spirit, she was also the mother of God's Son, who Joseph is to name Jesus.

The path for Joseph was genuinely unpredictable. The Holy Family was constantly moving–from Bethlehem, Egypt, Nazareth, and Jerusalem. They experienced exile from their homeland to Egypt. Twelve years later, they lost Jesus and needed to search for him over the course of three days, only to find Him in the temple. Through it all, Joseph stayed the course, no matter what. He was a righteous man.

Next time you are struggling to accept God's will in your life, think about St. Joseph. No questions asked, he habitually responded, "Yes, Lord," … and off he went again and again. Take the next step by bringing your struggle to Sunday Mass, and realize that when you pray the words of the Creed, you are making a profound Profession of Faith, a great "yes" to all that God has revealed, even if it is hard. This "yes" opens your heart to encounter Jesus in the great Sacrament of the Altar. And whenever you find this problematic–even if it is every time–know that St. Joseph, the patron of the Universal Church, is always silently waiting for you to ask for his help. Always be faithful; he will help you remain steadfast, even when it hurts.

# THURSDAY OF THE SECOND WEEK OF LENT
## MARCH 20, 2025

**READINGS**
Jeremiah 17:5-10
Psalm 1:1-2, 3, 4, 6
Luke 16:19-31

**REFLECTION**
Mother Teresa was not a woman of striking physical beauty. But her spiritual beauty was off the charts. Men and women, atheists and Christians alike, were magnetically drawn to her. She was just so good.

And how did she spend her days? Lifting the bodies of dying people from the gutters of Calcutta and bringing them to the home she'd established, where she would cleanse their sores not just with water and antiseptic but far more effectively with her love.

Many people know that Mother Teresa lived a deeply Eucharistic life. She spent hours each day in the presence of the Blessed Sacrament at Mass and in Eucharistic Adoration. She saw Jesus in the Eucharist, and therefore, she could see

Him in the distressing disguise of the poorest of the poor.

Today, Jesus tells the story of Lazarus and the rich man. Lazarus, the starving man covered in sores, was ignored by the man whose wealth was the sole occupation of his mind.

It wasn't until the rich man reached eternal punishment that he realized the grave error of his ways and expressed concern for his brothers, lest they share in his dreadful fate. But Abraham tells him that his brothers do not need extraordinary signs. The prophets have proclaimed all they need for salvation.

May we allow Mother Teresa to be a prophetess for us today so that our hearts may be open to the poor among us. As she testifies, it all begins with Jesus, truly present, albeit hidden, in the Holy Eucharist.

# FRIDAY OF THE SECOND WEEK OF LENT
## MARCH 21, 2025

**READINGS**
Genesis 37:3-4, 12-13a, 17b-28a
Psalm 105:16-17, 18-19, 20-21
Matthew 21:33-43, 45-46

**REFLECTION**
In the parable we hear at Mass today, the father says, "They will respect my son." God the Father entrusts His Son to us. How do we show respect to the Son of God?

The answer is simple: We can respect Jesus by making time for prayer each day— the Rosary, reading Scripture, or a few minutes in quiet gratitude. We respect the Son by attending Mass— coming on time, prepared, and open-hearted. We can review the readings before Mass so our hearts can receive God's wisdom. We can make time for Eucharistic Adoration at a local parish during the week to "fan the flame of faith" in our hearts, making us more eager to receive Jesus in communion. What is simple, though, is not always easy. Our human will can be weak, and there are often obstacles and distractions to our prayer.

Showing respect for the Son also requires that we care about the people Jesus cares about. Jesus tells us, "Whatever you did for these least brothers of mine, you did for me" (Matt 25:40). How do I "respect the Son" in people experiencing poverty, older people, and people experiencing homelessness? Is there one small action you can take to do this, Lent? Perhaps volunteering at a nursing home on a Saturday afternoon or donating to a pro-life pregnancy center? What is simple, though, is not always easy. Far too often, we tend toward a self-centered view of the world rather than seeing with the eyes of God and loving our neighbor.

Saint Paul often refers to the Church as the Body of Christ. We can "respect the Son" by loving and respecting the Church. If people criticize the Church, turn the conversation in a positive direction— what are the good things happening in our parish or Catholic school? Are we open to Catholic teachings on moral issues regarding marriage and family life? Am I familiar with what the Church teaches on these topics? Prayer and study can help us to understand the Church's wisdom on these topics. But again, what is simple is not always easy. Are we striving to grow in our knowledge of the faith to defend the Church, and do we have the courage to stand up and share truth when called upon, or do we find ourselves unprepared for the moment or too afraid to say anything?

Finally, as followers of Jesus, we want to do more than "respect the Son." We want to love Him. We want to welcome Him into our lives, homes, and hearts. He loves us, too! He wants to abide in my life, home, and heart. "They will respect my Son." This love is true simplicity, and it is something we can do now—we can be present to Jesus and allow Him to be present to us.

# SATURDAY OF THE SECOND WEEK OF LENT
## MARCH 22, 2025

**READINGS**
Micah 7:14-15, 18-20
Psalm 103:1-2, 3-4, 9-10, 11-12
Luke 15:1-3, 11-32

**REFLECTION**
Today, we hear one of the best-known parables in all of the Gospels: the parable of the prodigal son and his merciful father. This parable shows us the importance of conversion and repentance. In the parable, a son asks his father to give him his share of the estate he will inherit, and his father does so without asking for anything in return. The son runs off to a distant land, where he squanders his inheritance "on a life of dissipation." The prodigal son thinks he is gaining his freedom by leaving his home, but instead, he finds himself "longing to eat his fill of the pods on which the swine fed." His freedom is an illusion: by leaving his father, he has lost all that is meaningful and has been brought to the brink of death.

This man has discovered that true freedom comes from his union with his father: he realizes that even his father's servants are more fortunate than he is. He returns to his father to beg for a position as a servant. Without hesitation, the father responds to his son with mercy and love. We hear that while the son "was still a long way off, his father caught sight of him, and…ran to his son, embraced him and kissed him." The father throws a feast as a sign of his joy. We, too, are called to conversion and recognition of our failings, begging the Lord for His mercy. When we do so, our Father waits for us with open arms, ready to embrace us in his love.

The primary way we receive His grace is through the Sacrament of Penance and Reconciliation, where we receive pardon for all our sins. However, in the Eucharist, we are also nourished spiritually, strengthened in grace, and absolved of our venial sins. In the Eucharist, we are called to repent of our sinfulness and ask God for His mercy.

But there is another notable character in this parable: the older son, who becomes angry when he sees his father's tenderness toward his younger brother. The father gently rebukes this son for his coldness and tells him to rejoice at his brother's return. In the Eucharist, we are commanded to rejoice when someone repents and seeks the Father's forgiveness.

How many times in your own lives have you sinned or squandered the gifts that God has given you? Do we repent and return to the Father, asking for His forgiveness?

Have you been welcoming to others who have sought God's love and mercy? Have you avoided the envy and hatred that separates you from your heavenly Father?

# THIRD SUNDAY OF LENT
## MARCH 23, 2025

**READINGS**
Exodus 3:1-8a, 13-15
Psalm 103:1-2, 3-4, 6-7, 8, 11
1 Corinthians 10:1-6, 10-12
Luke 13:1-9

**REFLECTION**
Someone or something is always trying to get our attention. Our devices flood us with notifications: new messages, advertisements, emails, updates, warnings, news stories, game requests… and so on. Tiny screens flash with red "unread message" alerts, and our wrists buzz with a voicemail. We flip from app to app, video to video, from a large screen watching a game to a small screen when the commercials come on so we can watch short video snippets on our favorite social media platform.

Work is filled with people trying to get time and attention. Inboxes are flooded with meeting requests, follow-up emails, check-ins, and status updates. We receive direct messages from teammates via Slack, Teams, text messages, iMessage, and WhatsApp at all hours of the day.

It never stops, and perhaps reading through all of that just gave you a little bit of anxiety. It is unsettling when we step out of the daily routine of distraction. *We aren't meant to live like this.*

The greatest danger of distraction is that we can easily miss the ways God speaks to us. We may sometimes feel like God is silent or even absent, uncaring about our current situation. God is constantly working and speaking in our lives and world, but we are often too distracted to listen or care.

Consider the Gospel reading for today, which includes a unique exchange. Jesus speaks specifically about two events that would be fresh in the listeners' minds. This is one of the few places where Jesus references current happenings in the region, which are things people were discussing. Rather than speaking in a parable, Jesus uses the regional news to teach.

Our news is often sensational and fatalistic; we are drawn to drama. God cares deeply about current events and desires to communicate Himself through them, even tragic ones. Are we listening to God speaking? Are we attentive to how God desires to communicate Himself through our news, the events that unfold around us, and even the various movements of our day? Make no mistake: God can use every circumstance – good or ill – to communicate His glory and to teach us, even individually. This requires daily reflection, though. We must ask ourselves, "Where do I see God in this moment? What does God wish to speak to me here?" Apply this to your relationships. We often gossip about others, noting their failings and shortcomings. What if we used those moments to be convicted of our shortcomings instead? Rather than saying, "Wow, that person doesn't spend enough time with his or her kids. What a bad parent," we say, "Lord, I don't understand their situation. Please bless that family and help me recognize how I failed to be a good parent. Help me to repent of the ways I am falling short and show me how to do better."

This shift is not easy; it requires us to silence distractions to hear God speaking to us. In our First Reading today, Moses approaches God in the burning bush. What's intriguing here (aside from a burning bush that's not consumed) is that Moses needs to go out of his way to investigate the bush. The bush is not on his immediate pathway; Moses sees it *off* the path and approaches it. Imagine if Moses was distracted instead. He would have failed to see the fantastic thing happening and would not have profoundly encountered the Lord. He would not have heard God speaking and calling him. He would have continued on his way, unaware.

This is the choice we must make—to let go of distraction so we can hear God's call in our lives and, when we hear this call, to divert from our pathway so we can take time to listen.

One simple way we can do this through the rest of Lent is by making an intentional trip every day to the Eucharistic Adoration chapel or the space in front of the tabernacle at our parish. It may require diverting from our daily path and routine, driving some extra time, leaving for work a bit earlier, or rearranging our schedule. But even a stop of five or ten minutes each day can profoundly impact our faith. We approach the God of the Universe when we approach the Eucharist and remember that this is a far more profound encounter than Moses had with the burning bush. God used the bush as a sign to catch Moses's attention so that he could speak, but the bush was not God.

When we approach the Eucharist, we approach Jesus Christ – Body and Blood, Soul and Divinity – and we can listen, if we are not distracted, to His call. It is an encounter that puts us on holy ground, face-to-face with the Lord. Such a daily encounter would transform us, even if that encounter is just for a few moments.

# MONDAY OF THE THIRD WEEK OF LENT
## MARCH 24, 2025

**READINGS**
2 Kings 5:1-15ab
Psalm 42: 2, 3; 43:3, 4
Luke 4:24-30

**REFLECTION**
A foreign leader, Naaman was well respected and seemed successful in his work. Yet, he was a leper, considered unclean by many. His wife's servant, though she had been captured and taken from her home, thought that Naaman should visit Elisha to be cured of his leprosy. She offers him mercy and kindness despite his status as a foreigner and someone who had ripped her from her home. Almost equally surprising, Naaman listens to the girl and is given enough hope for a miraculous cure, so he seeks out his king and gets the king's blessing.

When Naaman sets out, he worships Rimmon (a Syrian deity sometimes known as Ba'al). He does not have any reason to seek out Elisha, a true prophet of the Lord, but he does so anyway. When Elisha hears about Naaman's desire to be cured, he convinces the king of Israel to allow him the opportunity to cure him as a sign that the Lord is truly God. He recognizes this moment as an opportunity to evangelize.

Elisha's instruction to Naaman to go to the River Jordan surprises the commander, who seemed to expect some magnificent ritual. But God's primary concern was healing Naaman's soul.

Again, Naaman is convinced to visit the Jordan and plunge into it. Once he is cured, he returns to Elisha, praises the Lord, recognizing for the first time the one true God, and proclaims this truth in front of his entire retinue.

This story is also a testament to God's work in our lives. We might expect rituals with tremendous deeds and words, but God uses the most basic elements to cleanse our souls and unite us with Him. In the simplicity of water, we are baptized and incorporated into the Mystical Body of Christ. In the Sacrament of Penance and Reconciliation, we are offered forgiveness for our sins through the simplicity of telling our sins to the priest and receiving absolution.

Most importantly, in the simplicity of the words of the Mass offered by the priest, God becomes present to us in a real and substantial way. He is there, veiled as bread and wine. Despite His humble appearance, how would we respond if he came to us with trumpet blasts and announcements like claps of thunder? How would we react if the bread changed physical form at the consecration?

Indeed, God could work in such marvelous deeds, but he also has something greater in store for us. How can we be receptive to his grace working in our own lives?

# SOLEMNITY OF THE ANNUNCIATION OF THE LORD
## MARCH 25, 2025

**READINGS**
Isaiah 7:10-14; 8:10
Psalm 40:7-8a, 8b-9, 10, 11
Hebrews 10:4-10
Luke 1:26-38

**REFLECTION**
We should approach the Feast of the Annunciation as a personal feast for each of us. This feast day reminds us that the Incarnation is not just a one-time event in the distant past but a continual reality. Jesus, God with us, is still with us, most especially in His enduring presence in the Holy Eucharist.

As we reflect on the Gospel today, we rejoice in the total cooperation of the Immaculate Virgin Mary, who, because she had never known sin, was able to give a free and complete response to God's will to bear Jesus in her womb and bring forth the Savior who will redeem us. Her acceptance to God through His word was so strong that the Word would take on her own flesh.

In response to the Archangel Gabriel's calling her *kecharitomene (the Greek word indicating that the action of giving grace has already occurred),* "You who have been filled with grace," she humbly referred to herself as "The handmaid of the Lord." To be full of grace — full of God's Divine Life like the Son she conceived - is to be also fully at God's service. Likewise, her body, soul, and spirit were fully and freely at God's disposal. Her response to God's word, God's will, and God's plans are held up to us each day by the Church as a model. The same Holy Spirit who overshadowed Mary in Nazareth and throughout her life comes now to overshadow the altars of our Churches and all of us in a double epiclesis.

First, He comes to work a great miracle changing bread and wine into His Body and Blood, Soul and Divinity. Then He wants to overshadow all of us and, through our communion with the Word-made-flesh, transform us into one body, one spirit in Christ.

# WEDNESDAY OF THE THIRD WEEK OF LENT
## MARCH 26, 2025

**READINGS**
Deuteronomy 4:1, 5-9
Psalm 147:12-13, 15-16, 19-20
Matthew 5:17-19

**REFLECTION**
Jesus came to fulfill the law, not to abolish it. The law is God's will for all we say, our attitude, and all we do. To fulfill the law, though, is not to go beyond the "rules" and restrictions but to live the love of God and love of neighbor that underpins the entirety of the law. Many people who listened to Jesus did not understand this; they believed that, so long as they did not murder someone, they were following the law. While true, the fulfillment of the law would be to love those around them, provide for their needs, and show hospitality and compassion.

We can fall into a similar way of thinking. When we go to Mass on Sunday, we follow the Church's precepts and fulfill our Sunday obligation. We are following the rules. But Jesus calls us beyond the regulations to the true fulfillment of the obligation. We fulfill the law by living as a Eucharistic Missionary. A Eucharistic Missionary is a Catholic who has experienced a personal encounter with Christ in the Eucharist and uses that experience to serve others. The "Eucharist commits us to the poor" and unites us more closely to the Body of Christ (CCC 1396-1397). Eucharistic Missionaries begin their journey by encountering Jesus in the Eucharist and receiving Him in Holy Communion. They are then sent forward to share the love of Christ with others. Our encounter with the Eucharist transforms our way of life, speaking, praying, and acting toward God and our neighbor; the corporal and spiritual works of mercy bring great joy to the life of a Eucharistic Missionary. When we live in this way, fulfilling the law in our lives, our parishes become sacred spaces in which every person is led to deeper communion with God and with their neighbors, and the places that we go to beyond our parish walls become places of sacred encounter where the love of Christ, in us, meets others.

# THURSDAY OF THE THIRD WEEK OF LENT
## MARCH 27, 2025

**READINGS**
Jeremiah 7:23-28
Psalm 95:1-2, 6-7, 8-9
Luke 11:14-23

**REFLECTION**
Sometimes, we don't want to see what is right in front of us.

Today's First Reading is a lament spoken on behalf of God by the prophet Jeremiah. The relationship the Lord desires with us is simple: Listen to my commands, and you will be my people. This divine reciprocity is simple, and we, the people, benefit in a double portion.

God's commands are not restrictive but liberating. To heed the voice of the Lord is to avoid self-inflicted pain and heartbreak. Walking in the way God sets before us allows us to be free of the many traps in the paths we choose when we go our own way. Furthermore, to be God's people is to enjoy the comfort of the Lord who can make all things work for our ultimate good – holiness. When there are moments of suffering and heartbreak that are not self-inflicted but merely a part of the human experience, God is present to comfort us. When we are in need, God is there to provide for us.

Throughout history, God has given the people this choice: Follow my commands and be my people, or choose your way at your own risk. He even sent prophets to call them back when they went astray. Jeremiah's lament should cut to our hearts—we are the people to whom He is speaking.

How often have we heard a "prophetic voice" calling us to holiness and to return to the Lord? Perhaps that voice was our conscience or the words of a friend. You may have seen something miraculous as the crowds did in the Gospel today. Yet, our hearts can be tricky. We ignore what is right before us and instead choose our own way.

God never tires of calling us; when His chosen people turned away, God pursued them through the incarnation and rescued all of us through His death and resurrection. The offer of eternal life and freedom is right in front of us. Today, may we have eyes to see it.

# FRIDAY OF THE THIRD WEEK OF LENT
## MARCH 28, 2025

**READINGS**
Hosea 14:2-10
Psalm 81:6c-8a, 8bc-9, 10-11ab, 14 and 17
Mark 12:28-34

**REFLECTION**
"Love the Lord with your whole heart," Jesus tells us in the Gospel today (Deut 6:4, Mark 12:30). This is the first and greatest commandment. How can we love the Lord with our "whole hearts?"

Our hearts have four chambers: the left atrium, the right atrium, and the right and left ventricles. One heartbeat is a complex and graceful movement. The heart muscle pumps blood from the body through the chambers of the heart, past the lungs, again through the heart, and back out to the body. Oxygen from the lungs refreshes the blood, giving us energy to feel, think, speak, and move. Our hearts beat every second of every day.

The biological necessity of the heart is a powerful metaphor for the vitality and life of a person. Just as a heart has four vital chambers, there are four essential areas from which our life flows: our emotions, thoughts, words, and actions. How can we love the Lord in each of these areas? In our emotions, we can bring our joy to the Lord, thanking Him for His blessings. We can also bring Him our sorrows– prayerfully asking for His help. We can ask the Lord to shape our thoughts according to His truth. Reading the Bible and the Catechism helps us to know and love God's teachings.

What about the words that flow from our hearts? Do we fall into cursing or negative criticism of others? Jesus speaks words of truth and love. We love the Lord "with all our hearts" by building up others instead of tearing them down. Finally, we're called to love God in our actions. Do we treat our families with love and warmth? Do we treat our enemies with mercy?

In the Sacred Heart of Jesus, the Lord offers us a model for our hearts. The different aspects of the Sacred Heart of Jesus are integrated, praising the Father with every heartbeat. Jesus offers His joys and sorrows to the Father. The Father's love and wisdom shape His thoughts and words. In His actions, Jesus praises the Father and shows mercy to each of us.

Our hearts are muscles, giving us strength for action. Jesus offers us a model in His Sacred Heart, shaping our hearts to be like His. In the Eucharist, He gives us His Body and Blood, Soul and Divinity, the food that strengthens our hearts to love as He loves.

# SATURDAY OF THE THIRD WEEK OF LENT
## MARCH 29, 2025

**READINGS**
Hosea 6:1-6
Psalm 51:3-4, 18-19, 20-21ab
Luke 18:9-14

**REFLECTION**
"O, God, be merciful to me, a sinner." This simple prayer in the Gospel reading is a profound expression of humility. For our reflection today, we can look to St. Francis, who uniquely embodied humility.

For St. Francis, the supreme witness for humility is the Sacrament of the Eucharist, and the Eucharist is not a static "thing" but a dynamic person who is present on the altar in a real and substantial way. At the end of his life, in his testament, St. Francis writes, "I see nothing corporally of the Most High Son of God except His most holy Body and Blood." The Real Presence to St. Francis was an intimate one. For Francis, his Lord and brother Jesus came to him personally whenever he received Communion.

Most astounding to Francis was how Jesus is present to us in the Eucharist. When the Word of the Father first came to us in the flesh, He did so in great humility and poverty. In fact, for Francis, the very act of becoming human reflected the humility of the all-powerful God. Although He is now glorified and seated at the Father's right hand, Jesus comes to us in even more humility and poverty, not only under the guise of ordinary bread but as food. In a letter to all the friars, St. Francis breaks into rapturous praise of the humility of the One who came to serve and still comes to serve: "O wonderful loftiness and stupendous dignity! O sublime humility! O humble sublimity! The Lord of the universe, God and Son of God, so humbles Himself that for our salvation, He hides Himself under an ordinary piece of bread! Brothers, look at the humility of God and pour out your hearts before Him!"

Our only possible response to such divine generosity and humility, St. Francis says, is to: "Humble yourselves that you may be exalted by Him! Hold back nothing of yourselves for yourselves, that He Who gives Himself totally to you may receive you!"

# FOURTH SUNDAY OF LENT
## MARCH 30, 2025

**READINGS**
Joshua 5:9a, 10-12
Psalm 34:2-3, 4-5, 6-7
2 Corinthians 5:17-21
Luke 15:1-3, 11-32

**REFLECTION**
God is doing something new.

The Eucharistic Life constantly seeks ways in which God is moving, speaking, and acting in our lives to bring renewal. The spiritual life is a progression; we are pilgrims on this earth, and the Lord desires us to journey with Him.

This requires us to hold everything loosely, ready to let go of our previous understandings, conceptions, and paradigms regarding our relationship with God. The spiritual life is a work of revelation; God is unchanging, but we are changing. We are growing, regressing, and growing again. When we hold onto our current relationship with God too tightly, we risk losing sight of God altogether.

If this seems strange, today, we need to look at the total movement of the readings. It is worth pausing here to read all four and sit with them for a moment. If you have not done this, do it now, and then return to the rest of this reflection.

Welcome back.

In the First Reading, consider the joy and pain of the moment for the Israelites. They are celebrating the first Passover in the Promised Land. The wandering in the wilderness of Sinai began with the Passover and exodus from Egypt, and now it ends with the Passover in the Promised Land. For years, God has fed the people with manna in the desert – a miraculous food that was a tangible sign of God's providence. There is something painful about this reading, like the pain a mother may feel when weaning an infant off breastfeeding or when a parent watches a child leave for college because the relationship has changed. "No longer was there manna for the Israelites." As joyful as this first Passover in the Promised Land was, there must have been some pain as the manna ceased.

The Gospel reading for this Sunday presents us with a story we have already heard once this Lent – a parable of two brothers. The main character we often miss is the older brother, who ends the parable standing outside of the father's house. To the audience listening to Jesus, the older brother is justified in his frustration. His father is not acting the way the older brother expects a father to act. This parable is scandalous to the people listening to Jesus because their mind is the same as the older brother's. This is not, culturally, how a father would act toward a prodigal son. The parable is a call that, like the older brother, we must recognize that we cannot fathom the depths of the mercy of God. It is a paradigm shift; God is unchanging, but our understanding of Him must change, or like the older brother, we will find ourselves standing outside of the house of the Father.

Saint Paul clarifies this in his second letter to the Church in Corinth: When we follow Jesus, we are a new creation and what is old passes away. This is not a one-time event, though – it is the journey of the pilgrimage. God constantly renews us, calling us to repent of sinful behaviors, attachments, and inaccurate understandings of Him.

Nothing on this side of heaven is the end game. Even the Eucharist is a foretaste of heaven, not the fullness of heaven. Like the manna in the desert, when we enter the Promised Land, we will not need the Eucharist anymore because we will be given the fullness of what the Eucharist promises. This reality, in itself, should convict us of holding everything – even the good things – with a loose hand.

# MONDAY OF THE FOURTH WEEK OF LENT
## MARCH 31, 2025

**READINGS**
Isaiah 65:17-21
Psalm 30:2 and 4, 5-6, 11-12a and 13b
John 4:43-54

**REFLECTION**
As we enter this fourth week of Lent following Laetare Sunday, we are given a joyful outcome based on the royal officer's desire for his son to live. The royal officer put his faith in Jesus' ability to heal, and Jesus healed his son. We are called to put our faith in God as we move forward in life, believing in the ways He has provided for us and revealed Himself to us.

In every Eucharistic celebration, we are offered this same call to faith. It is pure joy to receive the Eucharist as a sacrament that heals. "The man believed the word that Jesus spoke to him and went on his way." This is remarkable because the man had asked Jesus to come with him. But when Jesus spoke, "Go; your son will live," the man obeyed without a question. He believed and went. He did not insist on seeing the miracle. He did not complain that Jesus would not come with him.

Amazingly, he left, "believing." We can believe that in that moment of seeing Jesus speak so sovereignly, something awakened in man and can in us, too. He saw something more than a miracle-worker. A dying boy healed with a word, over distance, at once. Such is the power of Jesus. In receiving the Eucharist, we behold the Lamb of God. We behold His glory, and we have all received grace upon grace from His fullness. "Lord, I am not worthy that you should enter under my roof, but only say the word, and my soul shall be healed." May the Lord remove all pride, all unbelief, all self-reliance, and reveal to us the glory of the grace and power of Christ so indeed our soul shall be healed.

# TUESDAY OF THE FOURTH WEEK OF LENT
## APRIL 1, 2025

**READINGS**
Ezekiel 47:1-9, 12
Psalm 46:2-3, 5-6, 8-9
John 5:1-16

**REFLECTION**
Today's Gospel depicts a man paralyzed, desperate, and longing for healing. After 38 disease-ridden years, he chooses to hope in an unpredictable pool whose waters might reach him to alleviate his affliction. He was abandoned and without help in his efforts of rehabilitation, a man lying in the heartbreaking reality of a forsaken desire for restoration.

But then, Jesus saw him. In an encounter of love, He gazed upon this man who ached for revival. In that piercing gaze, Jesus came down to him and heard the cries of his heart. He responded with a question: "Do you want to be healed?" (John 5:6) At that moment, Christ desired that this man would assent to the healing that was only possible in the presence of the Word. And, so the man lying on the mat did.

"Rise, take up your mat, and walk" (John 5:8).

The man who was rejected, abandoned, and left to fend for himself at a pagan pool was seen and healed by the Font of Everlasting Life. Christ's healing inspired this new man to rise, walk to the temple, and worship in praise and thanksgiving. In an experience of mutual desire, the Messiah came to heal him of his physical and spiritual ailments, stirring him to rise to his feet and walk in the path of righteousness.

In our Lenten pilgrimage, the Holy Mother Church offers this Gospel as an invitation for us to make our needs known to Christ and allow Him to heal us. His Real Presence in the Eucharist heals our wounds of abandonment and rejection. He encounters us with His healing presence and reconciles us in the Body of Christ so that we may all rise and walk together on the path to eternal life.

This Lent, how will you respond to Christ's gaze as He asks you, "Do you want to be healed?"

# WEDNESDAY OF THE FOURTH WEEK OF LENT
## APRIL 2, 2025

### READINGS
Isaiah 49:8-15
Psalm 145:8-9, 13cd-14, 17-18
John 5:17-30

### REFLECTION
In today's Gospel, we find the Jews not only bewildered by the carpenter-turned-street preacher performing miracles on the Sabbath but enraged by His claim of being equal to God. They are stunned when He refers to the Lord as "Father." With Jesus' life seemingly on the line, how does this Nazarene respond to these men plotting to kill Him? He roots Himself in His identity as Son and testifies to the mission for which He was sent. He gives them a glimpse into the inner workings of Trinitarian communion, the love between the Father and the Son.

In the Infancy Narratives of his book "Jesus of Nazareth," Pope Benedict XVI states, "Jesus' freedom… is the freedom of the Son… As Son, Jesus brings a new freedom: not the freedom of someone with no obligations, but the freedom of someone united with the Father's will, someone who helps humanity to attain the freedom of inner oneness with God." Jesus came to set us free because He is free. This is the work of the Redeemer who steadfastly comes to save us, to show us the face of God, and reconcile us to our destiny. He raises us from our tombs of sin and death to transform our old hearts of stone into new hearts of flesh. He does this so that we may live in Him, with Him, and through Him. At His word and in His authority, He opens the grave, and we rise, free to live as sons and daughters of the Eternal Father.

To attain this freedom, we must first acknowledge and then consent to be delivered of our slavery and bondage. We must let Him save us from the treacherous state we are mired in. During this Lenten season, let us pray that we may surrender the dead parts of our hearts. May we offer these facets of our lives back to Him, who brings resurrection and freedom to those who, at the sound of His voice, rise to new life and follow Him.

# THURSDAY OF THE FOURTH WEEK OF LENT
## APRIL 3, 2025

**READINGS**
Exodus 32:7-14
Psalm 106:19-20, 21-22, 23
John 5:31-47

**REFLECTION**
We are tactile creatures. We rely on our senses to tell us what is real – what we can see, smell, taste, touch, and hear. We anchor ourselves in the physical experience of our world, which we call "reality." However, this presents a challenge for us because we are not merely physical creatures. We are also spiritual creatures, and there is a spiritual dimension to our world that is just as real as what we can see, taste, smell, hear, and touch.

But we are quick to rely on our bodily rather than spiritual senses.

In the First Reading today, Moses is conversing with God on Sinai, but the people have built an idol to worship. The idol was created because Moses was gone for a long time, and the people longed for something they could see and touch – a god that was "real." How often do we create these same idols in our lives, out of people, out of jobs, out of money? When the Lord seems distant, we craft something to worship.

It is easy to see the Israelites as faithless, but we are not far from their folly. Today, be mindful of the idols you create when God seems distant, when the voice of Jesus is faint, or when the power of the Holy Spirit feels like it has left you. In these moments, we will see comfort in the physical world, grasping at something to hold onto when we lose touch with spiritual reality. Thankfully, there is a remedy.

Run to the Eucharist. God gave us the sacraments as tangible, efficacious signs of His invisible grace. He created us as tactile creatures and provided us with material signs to help bridge the physical and spiritual world. These are humble signs, to be sure – water in baptism, bread and wine in the Eucharist, oil in anointings that occur in confirmation, anointing of the sick, and holy orders. Still, they communicate something powerful, something we can hold onto. When you feel the temptation to run to an idol, hoping to find reality, turn toward the Lord, present in the Blessed Sacrament, and worship Him and ground yourself in what is truly real.

# FRIDAY OF THE FOURTH WEEK OF LENT
## APRIL 4, 2025

**READINGS**
Wisdom 2:1a, 12-22
Psalm 34:17-18, 19-20, 21 and 23
John 7:1-2, 10, 25-30

**REFLECTION**
"What's your name? Where are you from?"

We may ask and answer these friendly questions when we meet someone new. Follow-up questions might include, "What's your profession? Where did you go to school?" At their most genuine, these questions are searching for common ground for a conversation or even a friendship. But sometimes, we wonder if people are not searching for common ground but evaluating us instead. We question if people are really asking: How wealthy are you? How smart? Are you worth my time?

In today's Gospel, Jesus tells the people, "You know me and also know where I am from" (John 7:28). They know Him but don't understand Him. They see Him as the son of Joseph, the carpenter from Nazareth. While this is true, it is not the whole truth. He is Jesus Christ, the eternal Son of the Father. Joseph is His adopted father, but Jesus is from heaven, born of the Blessed Virgin Mary. His "profession" is Messiah, the savior of the human race. He is one person with two natures, fully divine and fully human.

Recall Jesus' question to Peter, "Who do you say that I am?" (Matt 16:15). Jesus looks at Peter and engages him personally. Peter looks at Jesus and says, "You are the Messiah, the Son of the living God." The question is genuine, and the answer is authentic.

Today, talk to Jesus, perhaps in Eucharistic Adoration. We know Him, and we want to know Him more fully. From your heart, tell Him, "Jesus, for me you are…" You might call Him "savior, shepherd, friend, my Lord and my God." These titles are used at Mass and in Catholic prayers. Each title is proper, highlighting different aspects of His person, life, and mission. Thank Him, praise Him, love Him! He is worthy.

Continuing this conversation, let Jesus tell you who you are. You grew up in a particular city, attended various schools, and have a specific job. More profoundly, you are a "beloved son" or "beloved daughter" of God. You are a disciple of Jesus, His friend. We are sinners, yet Jesus offers us His forgiveness. You are worthy.

Jesus Christ, I want to know you more fully. Jesus, I want to be known by you. May my true identity be rooted in my relationship with you.

# SATURDAY OF THE FOURTH WEEK OF LENT
## APRIL 5, 2025

### READINGS
Jeremiah 11:18-20
Psalm 7:2-3, 9bc-10, 11-12
John 7:40-53

### REFLECTION
Jesus stands outside of our boundaries and beyond our expectations. Unfortunately, we are often so locked into a particular way of understanding Jesus that we become blind to the complete picture of who He is. In the Gospel reading today, an argument arises over whether Jesus is the Messiah. It is a scriptural argument; some members of the crowd believe that Jesus' place of origin disqualifies Him, based on scripture, as potentially the Messiah.

What is the lens through which you view Jesus? Do you see Him as a righteous judge? A faithful companion? A servant suffering in the poor? King of the Universe? High priest? Indeed, He is all of these and much more, but sometimes, our fixation on one aspect of Jesus can hinder our ability to see Him as another.

Maybe you see Him through a lens of brokenness or distrust, hurt by someone in the Church, or by an unanswered prayer. You may perceive Him through a lens of doubt or questioning. Our experience of Jesus can be distorted as a result of our interactions with people who claim to follow Jesus, people who are hurt and broken – sinful people.

A lens can create a bias, which is to the detriment of understanding and full relationship. The Pharisees held some bias against Galilee; not only do they refuse to accept that the Messiah might come from this region, but they give orders that "no prophet arises from Galilee."

Do you have a bias that is preventing you from knowing Jesus? How is this perspective distorting your understanding of the Lord? We correct our misunderstanding by spending more time with Jesus and simply being in His presence, without expectation and boundaries. A simple prayer, "Lord, help me know you more," opens us up to the mystery of Jesus without preconceived notions or biases and allows us to receive Him and to perceive Him in those around us.

# FIFTH SUNDAY OF LENT
## APRIL 6, 2025

### READINGS
Isaiah 43:16-21
Psalm 126:1-2, 2-3, 4-5, 6
Philippians 3:8-14
John 8:1-11

### REFLECTION
For today's reflection, we imagine ourselves in the Gospel Reading as individuals in the story. Close your eyes and put yourself there, close to Jesus, and listen to the story unfold. Feel the tension as the accusation is leveled, "This woman was caught in the very act of adultery."

We don't even get a name. We are told only her sin – "the woman caught in the act of committing adultery." That's who she is.

We can infer a few things about what is happening here to help us stay in our imagination and the moment.

The woman is caught in the act of adultery, so presumably, she is not fully clothed. A cloth or blanket has likely been wrapped around her to prevent scandalizing the crowd, but otherwise, she is naked. She is also alone; we are unsure of what has happened to the man, but the Law of Moses would require him to be killed as well. She is now a pawn in a bigger game while she awaits her fate. See the fear in her eyes, the loss of dignity... she stares only at the ground where she stands before Jesus, alone and ashamed.

The crowd wants to put Jesus into an impossible situation: Does Jesus, the compassionate one, follow the law of Moses and allow this woman to be killed? Or is Jesus a usurper of the law who will subvert the teaching of Moses and reveal His true colors? The crowd waits, tense. We wait, tense.

Jesus eludes the traps, though, and instead challenges us. He asks the crowds to reflect—are they innocent of sin, or have they simply not been caught? He asks the question and then kneels to write in the sand. Note that Jesus has not abandoned the woman; he remains with her as the crowd contemplates their next action.

Jesus always placed Himself near the broken. He laid down His life for the sinful, found solidarity with the poor, and sat close to those who wept.

The crowd walks away, with the oldest being the quickest to recognize their shortcomings. Jesus is then left alone with the woman as we look on. He asks her, "Woman, has no one condemned you?"

Pause here for a moment and let this line wash over you. Jesus does not speak her name, and we only know her as the "woman caught in the very act of adultery."

When Jesus calls to her after the crowd is gone, He simply calls her "woman." Jesus does not see her past but sees her future. No one has condemned her, and neither does He, but He does leave her with this call: Do not sin anymore.

This movement reveals to us a model of how we approach the world as missionaries. Jesus puts Himself close to the broken and, in this instance, stands close enough to them to feel the risk of pain. Do we do the same?

Jesus calls the sinful by their name, not their sin. Do we do the same for our enemies? For the people we dislike or disagree with? Do we give people the dignity of a name or bind them by describing their sin?

Jesus does not condemn the woman. Do we refuse to forgive others, or are we quick to pick up stones before we reflect on our lives and shortcomings? Do we thrive on the thrill of the punishment, hoping to see others "get what they deserve," or are we willing to forgo judgments, leaving those judgments for God alone and praying for them to repent?

To be sure, Jesus calls the woman to repent. Though the Lord does not call her by her sin, He loves her enough to call her away from her sin. Do we recognize that real mercy and compassion require us to call others to repentance so they can live free?

Only a person who has encountered Jesus can do this. Only a person who has been in the middle of the circle with Jesus, alone and afraid, can do this.

Perhaps you began this reflection from the perspective of a bystander, a crowd member, but that is not where you were.

You were the woman in the middle. You were the one Jesus saved. Jesus has found you in your sin and knelt by you, knowing your name and not merely your failures. He refuses to condemn you, and He refuses to let you remain bound by sin. Remain there with Jesus for a moment. Thank Him for what He has done for you. Go forward, sin no more, and give what you have been given.

# MONDAY OF THE FIFTH SUNDAY OF LENT
## APRIL 7, 2025

### READINGS
Daniel 13:1-9, 15-17, 19-30, 33-62
Psalm 23:1-3a, 3b-4, 5, 6
John 8:12-20

### REFLECTION
The beginning of the Gospel should be sufficient for us to reflect on today. It is the thesis statement for any saint, the hope of every Christian, the banner under which we live. Jesus is light in a dark world; following this light is to experience a full life.

Yet, when presented with this profound invitation, the Pharisees respond with cynicism and criticism. Jesus picks apart their arguments against Him: "You don't know me; if you did know me, you would understand me."

It is easy to be cynical in a dark world and to question and criticize. When something hopeful is shared with us, or we see the light in our parishes, our community, or our culture, we are quick to doubt the validity, and we wonder what is happening behind the scenes. We misidentify our cynicism as "wisdom," attributing it to our many years of life and living through similar circumstances. If we are not careful, we may find ourselves sitting in the seats of the Pharisees – cynical and critical of the work Jesus is doing.

If we know Jesus, though, our world is illuminated. We receive true wisdom – a gift of the Holy Spirit – and can perceive and see the world through God's eyes. Cynicism melts away in this light and allows us to live truthfully and judge rightly. When we walk in darkness, we must be cynical and test everything because we do not know what lies ahead of us. When we walk close to Jesus, we no longer need this disposition because we are confident He knows the way.

But it requires that we know Jesus through more than proximity but through vulnerability. It isn't enough to show up to Mass and go through the motions; we must come to the Eucharist ready to open our hearts to God ("lift up our hearts") so that we might sincerely know Jesus. When we do this, we welcome light in and no longer walk in darkness but experience the fullness of the life Jesus promised.

# TUESDAY OF THE FIFTH SUNDAY OF LENT
## APRIL 8, 2025

**READINGS**
Numbers 21:4-9
Psalm 102:2-3, 16-18, 19-21
John 8:21-30

**REFLECTION**
The crucifix is uncomfortable and a bit gruesome if you take a moment to think about it. It is not simply the cross, an instrument of execution and torture, but it bears the broken body of Jesus upon it. How many times do we pass by a crucifix in our home or at our parish and fail to grasp the weight of the image fully? Many other Christian denominations do not display the body of Christ on the cross. The reasoning, they say, is simple: Jesus came down from the cross and rose from the dead. There is no reason to keep the body there because this is only part of the story – the worst part. Why would we reflect on only half the story?

On the surface, this logic makes sense. But the purpose of the crucifix is not to stop only halfway through the story. To gaze upon the crucifix is to come to terms with the inevitable and ugly reality of death. The body of our savior, hanging broken on the cross, should evoke a pain in us... but also a joy. The fact of death – even death as gruesome and humiliating as death on a cross – leads to resurrection. We cannot skip past the reality of the crucifixion.

In today's First Reading, the people sin and experience punishment. Snakes are sent among them, inflicting fatal wounds. God, in His mercy, provides a remedy. If the people look at a bronze snake on a pole, they will be healed of any bite or wound inflicted by the serpents.

The people can be saved by gazing upon the serpent – the punishment for their sins – and coming to terms with this ugly reality. The bronze snake is a reminder that they must repent; their actions brought on the punishment.

The crucifix is this "bronze serpent" for us. We look on the cross and are moved to repentance, recognizing that our sins warranted such a punishment. Unlike the bronze serpent of Moses, though, we can look beyond the cross to the promise of eternal salvation and resurrection. We can see the love of God poured out, not as half the story, but as the part of the story none of us can avoid – death, pain, suffering. In looking up at the crucifix, we are moved to repent of our sins and find healing in God's mercy, which is displayed there and, finally, our hearts can be moved then to hope that just as the Father lifted Jesus up, so too will He lift us up, as well.

# WEDNESDAY OF THE FIFTH SUNDAY OF LENT
## APRIL 9, 2025

**READINGS**
Daniel 3:14-20, 91-92, 95
Daniel 3:52, 53, 54, 55, 56
John 8:31-42

**REFLECTION**
In today's Gospel, we find Jesus continuing to teach about His identity, and the people continue to struggle. We should take note of Jesus' words and the people's response, as St. John notes that Jesus is speaking "to those Jews who believed in him."

These are not the skeptics or the critics. These are the people following Jesus, who believe He is the Messiah. This is us.

Jesus tells the people that the truth will set them free if they remain in His word. The response? The people question Him — they have never been enslaved. How could Jesus free someone who is already liberated?

The debate continues, and Jesus reveals their hearts: He knows that, even though they "believe in him," there are many in the crowd that are seeking to kill Him. Jesus sees through their belief. It is fickle and not ready to stand trial and fire. Indeed, when Jesus enters Jerusalem before Passover, these same crowds will praise Him on entrance to the city, only to shout "crucify him" days later.

We can easily fall into this crowd.

The First Reading provides an example of the faith Jesus desires from us. Three men are threatened with death unless they worship a pagan god. The pagan king taunts them, asking if the God that these three men serve can deliver them from this death. The response of the men is one of bold faith and courage: If it is the will of God to save them, then they hope God will save them. But even if God doesn't save them, they won't turn from their faith.

They trust that whatever God wills for them is the best possible outcome.

Can we emulate that same faith? Can we display that radical trust that, even if the story doesn't go how we think it should, we will not turn our back on Christ? This precisely happens to the "believers" that Jesus addresses in the Gospel. The people want Jesus to overthrow the Roman government – they think He is a revolutionary. Jesus knows their hearts and knows that when the story doesn't go the way they want, this group will turn on Him and will turn Him over to that same government. As the season of Lent draws to its conclusion, may we be found in the furnace, tried by fire, and not in the crowds turning our back on our Lord.

# THURSDAY OF THE FIFTH SUNDAY OF LENT
## APRIL 10, 2025

**READINGS**
Genesis 17:3-9
Psalm 105:4-5, 6-7, 8-9
John 8:51-59

**REFLECTION**
Our lives are full of promises and commitments. Within relationships, commitments are often mutual – we promise a behavior to another person, and they promise one in return.

We commit to our company to show up to work and do what our job description says, and, in turn, our boss (and the company she represents) makes a commitment to pay us a specific amount of money, provide benefits, and (hopefully) treat us ethically.

We commit to our spouse to love and serve that person exclusively and uniquely and they make the same commitment to us.

Every year at Easter, we renew our baptismal promises, a set of commitments to God, and promise to reject sin and profess our belief in Jesus Christ and the Church He founded. We promise to live as disciples.

How well are we fulfilling our commitments?

The readings today focus on promises. God changes Abram's name and promises to make him a great nation. In return, God asks that Abraham and his descendants keep His covenant throughout the ages. In the psalm response, we sing, "The Lord remembers his covenant forever." Jesus tells the people, "whoever keeps my word will never see death." The picture painted is simple: The Lord desires our good and asks for a commitment to follow Him, listen to His word, and remember the covenant we've made with God through our baptism. In return, God offers us the very gift of Himself and the gift of eternal life.

God never forgets His commitment to us, but too often we forget our commitment to Him. When this happens, our love grows cold. Yet, God is merciful and faithful, even when we are not. As we approach Holy Week, take a moment to pray through the baptismal promises and renew them personally. Ask the Lord to revive your heart and remember His covenant; surely He will hear you, respond, and bring the renewal you seek.

# FRIDAY OF THE FIFTH SUNDAY OF LENT
## APRIL 11, 2025

### READINGS
Jeremiah 20:10-13
Psalm 18:2-3a, 3bc-4, 5-6, 7
John 10:31-42

### REFLECTION
We stand with Mother Mary. With her, we gaze at her Son with great love.

Mary sees the storm clouds gathering overhead. Jesus has spoken with the Pharisees. He has listened to them and responded to their questions. Their hearts have hardened, and Mary recognizes it. She loved Jesus and accepted this possibility. Through the archangel, Gabriel, God asked her to be the Mother of His Son. Mary says, "May it be done to me according to your word" (Luke 1:38). At this moment, Mary opened herself up to all that becoming the Mother of God would mean - including this painful moment.

Mary feels the air buzzing with electric tension. The Pharisees glance at one another, conspiring. The Roman soldiers shift their weight, edgy and nervous. Rough hands grip spears and swords. Perhaps Mary recalled the story of Passover, when God freed His people from slavery in Egypt through the prophet Moses. Jesus traveled to Jerusalem to celebrate the Passover with His disciples. Will Jesus try something to escape? If He does, the soldiers will be ready. Mary feels it. Jesus knows it. We see it.

In the Gospel today, Jesus asks, "For which of my good works are you trying to stone me?" (John 10:32). Mary closes her eyes, anticipating what happens next. Shouts, spears, condemnation, violence. Her son's death. She opens her eyes, seeing Him; once more, her heart is flooded with love for her son.

Conceived without original sin, united with His heart, it's as if she feels His emotions. His Heart is courageous and unafraid. He wants to pierce their hearts with the lance of truth. Will they listen? Will they receive Him? Will we? Mary held her newborn son years ago. She will hold Him again: lifeless and broken.

Today, on the edge of Holy Week, let us stay with Mary. Mother Mary, keep our hearts close to your Immaculate Heart. Amidst the violence and confusion, she remains faithful. She stays with Jesus in His passion, walking with Him. We want to stay with her and with her son. Lord Jesus, we ask to stay with you in your passion and death and to share in the glory of your resurrection.

# SATURDAY OF THE FIFTH SUNDAY OF LENT
## APRIL 12, 2025

**READINGS**
Ezekiel 37:21-28
Jeremiah 31:10, 11-12abcd, 13
John 11:45-56

**REFLECTION**
The Gospel leaves us with a cliffhanger on the edge of Holy Week. Jesus has raised Lazarus from the dead, and this is the breaking point for the religious authorities. Exorcisms, healings, and controversial teachings pushed the limit, but raising people from the dead was sure to get the attention of the people and, shortly after, the Roman authorities. The religious council decides to find a way to trap Jesus so they can execute Him and, hopefully, quiet His followers.

Jesus retreats for a while with His disciples, and, for a moment, heavy tension hangs in the air as the people wonder what will happen next. Jesus is in hiding; surely, He knows that His life is in danger. Will He let all of the excitement fade away and miss the Passover, or will He put Himself in the center of all the action?

We take a breath and wait because we know what will happen next. Jesus enters the final chapter of His earthly ministry, knowing what lies ahead is difficult but necessary.

There are moments like this in our lives.

We stand on the edge of challenge and difficulty, and we know what lies ahead.

The hard conversation.

The first step toward healing.

The last day at the job.

The counseling appointment.

We understand that these roads are marked by suffering but also hope – we enter the road knowing that there is life at the end of it. Jesus enters Jerusalem knowing there is resurrection, not just for Him, but for all of us.

What difficult moment have you been waiting to walk into? What is the hard but necessary road you need to take in order to experience healing, freedom, and a new life? As you stand there, know that Jesus stands with you, ready to carry that cross and walk the difficult road toward revival and renewal, even if it means suffering.

# PALM SUNDAY OF THE LORD'S PASSION
## APRIL 13, 2025

**READINGS**
Luke 19:28-40
Isaiah 50:4-7
Psalm 22:8-9, 17-18, 19-20, 23-24
Philippians 2:6-11
Luke 22:14–23:56

**REFLECTION**
Palm Sunday is the only Mass of the year at which we might hear the Gospel reading before the other readings, as we are accustomed to hearing them. At the beginning of our liturgy, we hear the story of Jesus' triumphant entry into Jerusalem as we wave palm branches and the priest processes toward the altar—just like the joyful crowds who waved palm branches as Jesus processed into Jerusalem.

We then resume Mass as normal and hear the Passion Narrative, also from the Gospel, in which Jesus sits at a table with His twelve closest friends and shares a meal with them.

We, of course, know that this isn't just any meal. This is the last meal He'll share with them before His arrest and crucifixion the following day. Today, we refer to this meal as "the Last Supper."

Jesus *knows* this is His last meal with His apostles.

So why does He tell them, "I have eagerly desired to eat this Passover with you before I suffer?"

Knowing what happens next, that is a bizarre thing to say. People don't desire to say goodbye to their loved ones, let alone eagerly want to do so. If anything, we dread doing that, and still more when it's our final goodbye. It's hard to imagine that Jesus was excited about saying farewell to His best friends, especially when He's so stressed and heartbroken that He sweats blood just a few verses later in this chapter.

*Jesus is excited to share this meal, not so He can say "goodbye," but so He can say "hello" in a different way.*

Jesus, the Word made flesh, has been anticipating this meal since the Fall of Man. He has been working toward this meal with every step of His public ministry. He has been setting it up with teaching and miracles. He has been praying about, strategically planning, and masterfully crafting this meal.

Why?

Jesus desires to give Himself to us in the Eucharist.

The Last Supper is the consummation of all of Jesus' teachings, Israel's history, and human history. After death entered the world through our eating of food from a tree (with Adam and Eve), God intentionally composed a plan to bring us life by eating food from a new tree (the Tree of the Cross).

*Of course*, Jesus eagerly desired to have this meal. *It's* part of God's master plan!

Today, we need to realize that if the Last Supper isn't this—if it's not the institution of the Eucharist—then it is a tragic event. Jesus' farewell to His friends is sudden and random, and His eagerness makes Him seem like an emotional masochist.

If, however, the Last Supper is this—if it's Jesus welcoming us into a new state—then the Last Supper is a night of joy. It is a night to be eagerly awaited. It is a night to celebrate, even if we know what lies ahead.

Today, we have more than one reason to rejoice. Not only did our Lord valiantly enter Jerusalem to face death head-on, but our Lord also gave us a gift that transcends time and space: He gave us Himself.

The next time we attend Mass, may we do so eagerly and ready to receive our Savior.

## MONDAY OF HOLY WEEK
### APRIL 14, 2025

**READINGS**
Isaiah 42:1-7
Psalm 27:1, 2, 3, 13-14
John 12:1-11

**REFLECTION**
Many economists claim that time has become our new currency. Our time is now the most valuable commodity we can offer in exchange for goods and services.
The adage is true: "Time *is* money."

Our culture is designed to keep us busy, distracted, and constantly in a state of frenzy. Breaking out of that built-in rhythm requires an intentional and conscious effort. Building a relationship with someone involves an investment of time, a very real value for us in the modern age.

Put another way, time with someone is a real gift.

When we spend time with Jesus in Eucharistic Adoration we give Him a real gift.

In today's Gospel reading, Mary Magdalene gives us one of the best examples of adoration and what it means to give to Jesus.

Mary hosts Jesus for dinner six days before His crucifixion with her siblings, Martha and Lazarus. Not knowing what lies ahead for Jesus but wanting to show Him love, she pours an expensive perfumed oil on His feet. How expensive is this oil? The cost is about "three hundred days' wages," which upsets at least one of the disciples.

There was no immediate return on investment for Mary of Bethany by doing this except for knowing that she honored our Lord.

Every time we go to Eucharistic Adoration, we act like Mary. We sit at Christ's feet and give Him the invaluable gift of our time. For others who misunderstand our relationship with the Lord, this may seem like a waste, just as pouring the oil over Christ's head seemed like a waste to Judas. However, Jesus is never outdone in generosity. Our gift of time in adoration is never wasted, and our honoring of Jesus is never without fruit.

On this Monday of Holy Week, let us dare to "waste" time with the Lord, knowing that our investment only brings about a greater return.

# TUESDAY OF HOLY WEEK
## APRIL 15, 2025

**READINGS**
Isaiah 49:1-6
Psalm 71:1-2, 3-4a, 5-6ab, 15 and 17
John 13:21-33, 36-38

**REFLECTION**
Many of the spiritual masters of our faith, the saints, have likened prayer to "oxygen for the soul." Just as our bodies need oxygen to live, our souls need prayer.

Prayer is essential to our spiritual life and growth.

Paragraph 2558 in the Catechism of the Catholic Church summarizes our relationship with Jesus as our prayer.

To put it bluntly: We're designed to pray.

But prayer can be challenging. Not knowing what to do can be daunting and stressful if we're unsure that we're doing it the "right way."

Breathing comes instinctually, so why does praying have to be so complicated?

In today's Gospel reading, the beloved disciple John provides a helpful and simple image of prayer. When Jesus announces that one of His disciples will betray Him, the disciples naturally want to know who it will be.

Peter cues John to investigate further, so John "leaned back against Jesus' chest" and asked Him who the betrayer would be. He then listened as Jesus explained that Judas would be the one to betray Him.

John rested near Jesus' heart and conversed with Him. This is prayer in its most authentic form.

When we pray, we quiet ourselves and speak with our Creator. We "lean back against" Him, humbly recognizing our dependence on His grace. We share with Him what's on our minds—all the things that bother us, excite us or confuse us. Like John, we can also bring others' concerns to the Lord.

Then, we listen for a response.

That's it.

Prayer is a quiet conversation, a restful back-and-forth with the Almighty. It raises our eyes to God and meets His gentle gaze as He looks down on us.

Spend some time today in this quiet conversation. Lean back against Jesus and fill your spiritual lungs.

# WEDNESDAY OF HOLY WEEK
## APRIL 16, 2025

**READINGS**
Isaiah 50:4-9a
Psalm 69:8-10, 21-22, 31 and 33-34
Matthew 26:14-25

**REFLECTION**
Many of us know the pain of betrayal from someone close to us. It's an excruciating experience.

Scans have shown that heartbreak has the same effect on our brains as withdrawal from hard drugs. When Jesus suffers in the Garden of Gethsemane before His arrest, He goes through the equivalent of the most wretched withdrawal humanity has ever known.

Jesus experienced more than heartbreak; He was betrayed at the expense of His life. Today's Gospel gives us a view into this infamous sellout.

To fully understand why Judas did what He did, though, we must return to Jesus' famous "Bread of Life Discourse" in the

Gospel of John, when He taught about the Eucharist.

In John 6, Jesus teaches about the Eucharist and the necessity of His flesh as food for the world. This is a hard teaching, causing the Jewish crowds to dispute amongst themselves and even forcing some of Jesus' own followers to leave Him. Many of us might be familiar with the tragic verse of John 6:66, when—for the only time recorded in the Gospels—many of Jesus' disciples "turned back and no longer went about with Him."

The teaching of the Eucharist served as a pivot point for discipleship with Jesus.

At the end of John 6, Jesus announces to His twelve apostles (His closest disciples) that one of them will betray Him. For the first time in the Gospels, Judas is mentioned explicitly as the one who will do this.

It's crucial for us to recognize that Scripture mentions Judas' betrayal when Jesus discusses the Eucharist.

The betrayal of Judas perhaps began in John 6, when Jesus spoke about the Eucharist. Before the Last Supper, Judas received an offer to hand Jesus over. Tragically, after the Last Supper, Judas goes through with the plan in complete betrayal. Venerable Fulton Sheen once said, "The beginning of the fall of Judas and the end of Judas both revolved around the Eucharist."

As was the case for all those following Jesus 2,000 years ago, our belief in Christ's Presence in the Eucharist is a decision point on our loyalty to Him. If we hold back on this teaching, we inevitably hold back other areas of our hearts.

Jesus staked everything on His teaching about the Eucharist in John 6 and gave everything in the Eucharist today in Matthew 26. May we strive to give Him everything in return.

# HOLY THURSDAY - EVENING MASS OF THE LORD'S SUPPER
## APRIL 17, 2025

### READINGS
Exodus 12:1-8, 11-14
Psalm 116:12-13, 15-16bc, 17-18
1 Corinthians 11:23-26
John 13:1-15

### REFLECTION
On this night, roughly 2,000 years ago, the world and our lives forever changed with the Institution of the Eucharist. Yet, the readings at the Holy Thursday liturgy spark some questions.

Why does our Gospel reading today focus on Jesus washing His disciples' feet? At first glance, it feels like a missed opportunity to reflect on and remember the Eucharist.

Why does the priest only wash feet at Mass once per year when Jesus makes it very clear that the disciples "ought to wash one another's feet" and again, "I have given you a model to follow, so that as I have done for you, you should also do?" It feels like the action doesn't really do what Jesus told us to do.

To answer these questions, we must look deeper to discover what the Church is trying to show us with today's Gospel reading.

Every time we serve our neighbor, we wash their feet. Every time we give food to people experiencing homelessness, we wash their feet. Every time we visit the elderly, we wash their feet. Every time we evangelize, we wash another person's feet.

Every time we bring someone to Christ, we help cleanse their feet from the paths they've trodden and set them on the pure path of Christ.

The work of "feet washing" both precedes and flows from our reception of the Eucharist. We cannot approach the table of the Lord if there is separation from our neighbor or divisions among us. Jesus preached against this, as did St. Paul (Matthew 5:23-24, 1 Corinthians 11:17-34). We are given these readings because they help us understand the mission we are tasked with when we sit at the table of the Lord.

This is why we're dismissed at the end of every Mass with something like "Go forth, proclaiming the Gospel by your life." Put another way, we are told to "Go wash the feet of the world."

May we do so with boldness, knowing that every pair of feet is precious to our Lord and no pair of feet is beyond His cleansing grace.

# GOOD FRIDAY OF THE LORD'S PASSION
## APRIL 18, 2025

**READINGS**
Isaiah 52:13–53:12
Psalm 31:2, 6, 12-13, 15-16, 17, 25
Hebrews 4:14-16; 5:7-9
John 18:1–19:42

**REFLECTION**
It's all led up to this. Here we are at the Passion of Jesus. We traveled with Him during Lent. We've been dreading this day. We're here, but we're not alone.

We are familiar with the movements of this day: There is the sham trial. The crowds shout, "If he were not a criminal, we would not have handed him over to you" (John 18:30). Is this the best they can do? An innocent man is convicted, condemned, and beaten. Marched to a hilltop, He will die a humiliating and painful death. Pilate had an opportunity and could have been a true hero, an early saint. He could have challenged the mob. He chooses his prestige instead. They yell, "If you release him, you are not a Friend of Caesar" (John 19:12). He bows to the mob's threats.  Mighty Pilate is a coward.

Amidst the violence, deception, suffering, and death, let us look to the Heart of Jesus. In our Good Friday liturgies, we see Jesus' love poured out for us. He holds nothing back, loving us to the cross. In His passion, we see His love received and shared by others, especially His mother.

Mother Mary encounters Him, beholds Him, and loves Him. In a brief but powerful embrace, her heart is united with His. He is not alone. Holy Mary, pray for us to remain faithful to Jesus despite pain.

Simon of Cyrene helps Jesus carry His cross. At first, he is reluctant, protesting and complaining. Then, walking with Jesus, Simon's heart is stretched, brightened, and converted. Lord Jesus, we want to walk with you, knowing that you walk with us, helping to carry our crosses.

The soldiers rest for a moment, and Veronica breaks through the crowd. With clean linen, she wipes Jesus' face, removing the dirt, sweat, and blood. Lord Jesus, renew your image in me; cleanse me of my sins through your passion.

The women of Jerusalem weep for Him. Carrying their children, they see Him as the Son of God and the son of Mary. Lord Jesus, with deep compassion, help me weep for my sins and the world's sins. Lord, you alone can heal us and redeem us.

Finally, at the foot of the cross, we gather with Mother Mary, her sister, John, Mary Magdalene and Mary, the wife of Clopas. Jesus is not alone. He looks at us, His Sacred Heart burning with love for us even as He hangs upon the cross. He breathes His last. Then, the soldier pierces His side with a lance as blood and water pour forth. The saints see this as an image of the sacraments of the Church, flowing from the very Heart of Jesus– water pours out in baptism and His Blood in the Eucharist. We are not alone; Jesus is with us.

At the cross, gaze upon Jesus, our Lord and Savior. Let us speak from our hearts. Thank Him, praise Him, love Him.

# HOLY SATURDAY - EASTER VIGIL
## APRIL 19, 2025

**READINGS**
Genesis 1:1–2:2
Psalm 42:3, 5; 43:3, 4
Romans 6:3-11
Luke 24:1-12

**REFLECTION**
When the sun goes down on the Saturday before Easter Sunday, the Church celebrates the holiest Mass of the year—the Easter Vigil. It's a long and beautiful liturgy during which we recount the story of salvation, welcome new members into the Catholic Church, and rejoice in our risen Lord. It is worth every minute.

Today's Gospel reading from the Easter Vigil Mass is beautiful for us to reflect on as we wrap up our Lenten journeys together.

When Mary Magdalene, Joanna, and Mary, the mother of James, announce to the apostles that Jesus' tomb is empty, they're met with pessimism. The apostles thought their story was not only improbable but "nonsense."

But Peter got up and ran to the tomb. He left amazed at what he found there—or the lack thereof.

Jesus appeared to Peter and then Peter told the other apostles that Mary Magdalene and the women were telling the truth. His witness and amazement likely chiseled at the doubts of the other disciples so that when Jesus finally appeared to them, they could fully believe.

This account shows us that it only takes the faith of a small group of people— even the shaky faith of someone who denied Jesus in his most dire moments – to inspire others.

It only takes the faith of a few… or even just one.

Many of us might feel like the only people in our families or friend groups who take the faith seriously. But it only takes one person to respond boldly for the Lord to do His work and bring them back.

Many of us might feel like the only person in our parishes who really cares that Jesus is there in the Tabernacle. But it only takes one person to respond with faithfulness and perseverance for the Lord to show up powerfully.

Some of us might doubt that the Lord is doing anything or will do anything with this Eucharistic Revival movement. But it only takes one person to respond with hope and love for the Lord to change our world forever.

Some of us see someone else's faith standing alone and wonder if we should stand with them. Remember, the women brought the good news of the resurrection back, and Peter used his authority to validate their claim. There are moments when we need to stand with others and share our faith.

We can stand with the new pastor who is trying to inspire Eucharistic faith but is being met with resistance from the congregation because he is "trying to do things differently than we've always done them."

We stand with the relative who recently converted to the faith and faces the exact resistance we have encountered.

Or with the youth minister who is desperately trying to find volunteers to lead young people toward Jesus but keeps hitting dead ends.

Sometimes, we are the ones who stand first in faith, and sometimes, we need to stand with those who are already moving in faith. So get up and respond, even if you have shaky faith.

Decide to chase after Jesus. Choose to trust His ways, no matter the cost. Commit never waver from Him.

It only takes the faith of one. Let it be yours.

# EASTER SUNDAY OF THE RESURRECTION OF THE LORD
**APRIL 20, 2025**

**READINGS**
Acts 10:34a, 37-43
Psalm 118:1-2, 16-17, 22-23
Colossians 3:1-4
John 20:1-9

**REFLECTION**
Happy Easter! He is risen, alleluia!

Today, we celebrate the anniversary of the most crucial day in human history: the day Jesus rose from the dead and conquered sin once and for all. Alleluia!

In today's Gospel reading at Mass, we hear how Mary Magdalene "ran and went to Simon Peter" after encountering the resurrected Jesus. She was overcome to share the most significant news ever told.

Let's pause there.

Mary Magdalene could have walked to Peter. She could have even walked *briskly.*

She could have skipped for joy or sat and prayed in gratitude.

But she *ran.* She couldn't contain herself with how utterly cosmic-shifting and perspective-altering Jesus' Resurrection is.

This is an essential detail for us to reflect on. Mary Magdalene recognized that Jesus' rising to new life changed things, and she moved with a sense of urgency and determination to share that news. Not only was Jesus indeed who He claimed to be, but we now had access to God like never before! We had access to eternal life!

When reminded of the Resurrection at Mass today, we might think it's nice that Jesus rose from the dead. We might even become overjoyed and grateful to Him for doing that — indeed, good and proper things to feel on this special day.

But we need to remind ourselves, right here, right now, that the Resurrection is *world-changing news.*

If we allow the Resurrection to change our worldview and affect our daily lives, we can become a source of new life for others. If we really understand the impact of what we celebrate today, we will naturally move with a sense of urgency and determination to share this news with the world.

And how do we do that? How do we allow this news to take root in our lives and seep into our pores?

You guessed it: The Eucharist.

Today at Mass (and at every other Mass), we're not simply celebrating the anniversary of Jesus' Resurrection: We're made *present* to His Resurrection. The empty tomb descends upon us, and we're beside Mary Magdalene!

Not only that, but we have the honor of allowing the resurrected Jesus to enter our hearts. There, we can encounter Him, be strengthened by Him, and be brought back to life.

At the end of Mass, when we're told to "Go forth," we have a decision to make. Do we saunter back to our routine? Do we walk back to those around us as if nothing has changed? Or do we *run* with renewed hope? With renewed resolve?

When Mary Magdalene encounters the resurrected Jesus, she runs back to Peter.

When Mother Mary conceives Jesus in her womb, she goes "*with haste*" to her cousin, Elizabeth.

When the two disciples on the road to Emmaus encounter Jesus in the breaking of the bread (the Eucharist), they return to the apostles "*at* once."

When people intimately encounter Jesus in Scripture, they *move with intentionality*. At Mass, when we encounter Jesus in the most intimate way possible, may we, too, be inspired to move with vision and clarity. We're not just called to run; we're called to run to someone in particular.

There is someone in your life right now whose world needs to be changed, whose life needs to be brought back to life. There is someone in your life who Our Lord wants to encounter through you right now. He wants to enter their emptiness and give them new hope.

But God needs you to run to them, intentionally pursue them, and recognize that you are His Plan A for that person!

Whether meeting up for coffee, bringing over some fresh-baked cookies, or a simple phone call to check in, trust the Holy Spirit to guide you in how exactly to "run" to this person.

We have world-changing news, brothers and sisters, and we cannot keep it to ourselves. He is risen, alleluia!

## ABOUT THE NATIONAL EUCHARISTIC CONGRESS

The National Eucharistic Congress was founded in response to the United States bishops' call for a National Eucharistic Revival. Its mission is to renew the Church by enkindling a living relationship with the Lord Jesus Christ in the Holy Eucharist.

Through impactful events, resources, and devotional books such as the one you are holding, the National Eucharistic Congress seeks to foster a movement of Catholics across the United States who are healed, converted, formed, and unified by an encounter with Jesus in the Eucharist—and who are then sent out on a mission "for the life of the world."

You can learn more about the National Eucharistic Congress and how to join this movement at eucharisticcongress.org.

# ABOUT THE AUTHORS

*Jane Guenther*

Jane is the Director of the Catholic Renewal Center for the Archdiocese of St. Louis. She has a degree in Architecture Education and acquired her Master's in Divinity in 2005. She is a spiritual director and teacher and served on the International and National Service Committee of the Catholic Charismatic Renewal. Jane currently serves on the Executive Advisory Committee for the National Eucharistic Revival. With Senite, Jane led the prayer partners and intercessory team for the National Eucharistic Congress and Revival.

Reflections: March 25, 26, 29, 31

*Tanner Kalina*

Tanner is the National Eucharistic Congress's mission outreach manager and has served with numerous missionary and ministry organizations spreading the Gospel. He is the co-creator of the Saints Alive podcast, which aims to bring the stories of the saints to life. Tanner speaks to groups of all sizes and ages about discipleship and the Eucharist and currently resides with his wife in Denver.

Reflections: April 13, 14, 15, 16, 17, 19, 20

### Zachary Keith, Ph.D.

Zachary earned his Ph.D. from the School of Theology and Religious Studies at the Catholic University of America. He is the Assistant Director of the Secretariat of Evangelization and Catechesis at the USCCB and enjoys spending time with his wife and four wonderful children. Zachary served as the doctrinal reviewer on this devotional.

Reflections: March 22, 24

### Fr. Joe Laramie, SJ

Fr. Laramie was a Eucharistic National Preacher and national director of the Pope's Prayer Network [Apostleship of Prayer]. He now directs Sacred Heart Jesuit Retreat House in Colorado. He is the author of "Love Him Ever More: a 9-Day Personal Retreat with the Sacred Heart of Jesus, based on the Spiritual Exercises of St Ignatius Loyola."

Reflections: March 7, 14, 21, 28; April 4, 11, 18

### Senite Sahlezghi

Senite is a consecrated virgin of the Archdiocese of Denver. Native to Colorado, she is a first-generation Eritrean American, a Licensed Professional Counselor with a master's in counseling psychology, and the School Counselor for St. John Paul the Great Catholic High School. Together with Jane, Senite led the prayer partners and intercessory team for the National Eucharistic Congress and Revival.

Reflections: April 1, 2

## Joel Stepanek

Joel is the Vice President of Programming and Administration for the National Eucharistic Congress and has served parishes and dioceses in ministry for 20 years. He holds a Master of Arts degree in religious education with an emphasis in youth and young adult ministry and a Master of Science degree in organizational leadership. Joel is an international speaker, author, and member of the Executive Advisory Committee for the National Eucharistic Revival. He lives in Phoenix with his wife and three children.

Reflections: March 5, 9, 16, 23, 27, 30; April 3, 5, 6, 7, 8, 9, 10, 12

## Sr. Alicia Torres

Sr. Alicia is a member of the Franciscans of the Eucharist of Chicago. She earned her Bachelor of Arts in Theology at Loyola University Chicago, an Master of Divinity degree at the University of St. Mary of the Lake/Mundelein Seminary, and a Master of Arts in Teaching at Dominican University. In addition to participating in the apostolic works of her religious community, she has been honored to serve the National Eucharistic Revival in many ways since 2021.

Reflections: March 6, 8, 10, 11, 12, 13, 15, 17, 18, 19, 20